To Suma,
May all your dreams
come true!! :)
Colleen O'Neill
zcolleen@yahoo.com

Writing Your Future

The Easy Way to Achieving Your Dreams

By

Colleen O'Neill

Heart World Books

Changing the world, one book at a time

Our Mission: To enrich the lives of our readers and help ease the suffering of humanity by giving generously of our profits.

Your heart has to first feel compassion before you will consider reaching out to help another human being. Our goal is to publish inspiring books to make our world a better place and to give to those in need.

Writing Your Future is a registered Trademark

Library of Congress Control number
2007926145

O'Neill, Colleen
ISBN Paperback 978-0-9795252-0-9

Heart World Books
First printing November 2007
Printed on acid free recycled paper.

Contents

Part Three: Overcoming Obstacles

Part Four: Creating more money

Part Five: Giving back to maximize success

Part Six: Summary of how to make it happen

Part Seven: Conclusion

About the author and the purpose of this book

My dream is to teach an easy goal writing method designed to give others the tools to have the life they design. I'm a real estate broker, home renovator, music therapist, and writer. My life's passion is making "cosmetically challenged" things beautiful.

In 1998 I first heard about Operation Smile, a charity that helps children who have facial deformities, when I saw Dr. Magee and his wife Kathy on television. Afterward, I wrote in my journal, "Someday I want to be involved with Operation Smile." Due to my financial situation at that time, I didn't begin donating until 2001. It was years later when I ran across my journal entry and realized how powerful my words were. It took three years to happen, but it did happen.

In the past few years, I have become personally acquainted with the founders Dr. Bill Magee and his wife Kathy. Their dedication to changing the faces and lives of children around the world inspires me.

Without a normal looking face, it's very difficult for a child to eat normally, or to even step outside their home for fear of ridicule. I want every child to have a chance at living life without isolation and shame. The surgery costs $240 for each child. In order to help 10,000 children, my publisher and I have set a goal of selling 2,400,000 books by Dec 31, 2012 and donating one dollar per book.

Dedication

I dedicate this book to you and to the fulfillment of your dreams. May the tools contained inside these pages help you make a difference in your life, and in the future of our world.

This book is also dedicated to the children throughout the world whose facial deformities are waiting to be surgically corrected through an Operation Smile mission. Help is on the way!

I would like to thank everyone who has ever helped and encouraged me. Especially my parents.

A note from the author

I believe that we all have limited time to read self-improvement books and to implement the ideas we read about. Because I value your time, this book shall be free of pages of tree robbing material and fluff that ultimately can confuse and overwhelm the reader.

I promise to give you steps on how to achieve your wildest dreams, plus actual stories of people who used the power of writing to create their future. This method requires very little time and no complicated steps to remember.

So read, and write on!

Colleen O'Neill

Introduction

Your dreams can come true. But before your dreams can come true, you have to know what your dreams are. What things do you want to possess? What gets you excited? What would get you up early each day? What gives you a sense of purpose in your life? What would you like to accomplish in your lifetime? What would your ideal life look, sound, and feel like if your dreams came true?

The ideas contained in this book are a composite of my own ideas and those of different thinkers and doers, many of whom will be quoted in this book. These concepts have been tested over many years and you can trust that they will work for you as well.

I wrote a shorter book because I believe if there are too many steps, the temptation is to read the book (if you finish it at all!), and then to do nothing. This book will help you clarify your goals and allay your fears about taking action. So grab a pen, a pencil, or a computer, and start writing your future!

> **"Some people dream of success while others wake up and work on their dreams."**
> Colleen O'Neill, author

The importance of a balanced life

It's not always easy to live a balanced life. But once you have set an intention to do so, you are on the first step toward the achievement of that goal. Accumulating money and possessions, or having a self-absorbed mentality should not be your only reasons for achieving your goals. You may accomplish them, but the end result could leave you feeling empty in some way. Your goals must be compatible with your values. Don't choose your goals based on what parents, peers, and society pushes you to do. If your dream is not something that you value, it is not one you will likely reach.

Having a sense of balance in the seven life areas of money, career, health, love, life dreams, fun, and spiritual pursuit will help you to achieve a fulfilled life. Getting enough sleep and having healthy habits like good nutrition and exercise will give you the foundation for making your dreams come true. Be sure to schedule time for fun. This will help give you the "fuel" to pursue your goals.

Sharing your abundance with others and spending time with friends and family will ultimately be the true road to living the life of your dreams. By spending just five minutes a day Writing Your Future, you will discover that living a balanced life can unfold one intention, one word, and one action at a time.

How I discovered writing the future

In 2004 during a move, I came across an old real estate training notebook. As I leafed through the pages I came to a writing exercise I took part in at a real estate conference in January 1994.

The instructor had asked us to write about our life in the present tense, as if it were already happening. The catch, he said, was to pretend it was really Dec 31, 1994, over 11 months from the date we were writing. We were instructed to write what our ideal life looked like, making sure to get into the feeling, seeing, and believing mode.

As I recalled that writing exercise of 10 years before, I sat down in shock after I read through my notebook. Nearly everything I had written had come true! In fact, the only item that didn't materialize was the amount of money I said I had made.

Here's what I had written

It's Dec 31, 1994 and I'm really enjoying the crackling fire in the fireplace of my first home. I'm playing my beautiful black baby grand piano that fits in the corner of my living room. I just opened my mailbox to find the rent check of my tenant living in the lower level. They always pay on time and they are so quiet. It's great having them here. They even put out the garbage cans most of the time. I have a wonderful new boyfriend. He is very good looking, kind, and athletic. He's a real estate agent too! I earned twice what I made last year. A great year for my 3rd year in real estate.

Here's what happened in real life

My goal to double my yearly income did not happen. I did earn more money than the year before, but not close to double my previous income. In all honesty, I did not work my business the way I knew in my heart would be necessary to achieve my goal. I was amazed, however, that I DID buy my first home by the date I had written.

In November 1994, I tried to obtain a home loan and was told I didn't qualify. I was initially very discouraged as I had a mental goal of having an accepted real estate contract on my first home by my birthday of December 17th.

That December, an agent in my office told me about an older client who wanted to sell her house. I made an offer on the house asking the seller to carry the financing. She accepted my offer on my birthday. I ended up closing escrow one day before the Dec 31, 1994 date I had written 11 months before! I had also started dating a real estate agent. He was just as I had described him. We were still dating on Dec 31st.

The house I purchased did not have an apartment when I bought it. One year later I built an apartment in the basement. The tenants were exactly as I described. They were quiet, paid rent on time, and they either set out the garbage on the day assigned or they brought back the empty cans later in the day. I did not have a piano when I moved in but I did buy a black baby grand piano five months later. The piano fit perfectly into the corner just as I had described. The house even had a fireplace.

As I read through these goals, I was amazed by a writing exercise that was so easy and produced such astounding results. I was only sorry I had not written more! I recalled at the time of the writing that what had stopped me from writing more was fear. I didn't want to write too many things because I thought I would just be depressed if they didn't happen.

So having my dreams come true was about wanting them to come true, and believing this was possible. The instructor told us not to get hung up on HOW it would happen. We were just to write about our lives as if the events were currently happening.

When I wrote my future, I really felt the feelings I would feel if I had achieved my goals. Pretending it was all real added passion to the writing as I wrote it. After that real estate conference, I don't recall ever re-reading what I wrote.

The wonderful aspect of Writing Your Future is that it works even if you don't have a lot of money or influential contacts. At the time I made the offer, I had only about three hundred dollars in the bank. I had tried to get a loan at a bank and was turned down. My vision of owning my first home was so strong that I believed I could somehow get the money for the down payment. I was owed $6,500 from the real estate company where I was working but I wasn't to be paid until weeks later. I needed the money that day, not in two weeks! Two hours before I had to sign papers on my new home, the company owner paid me the money he owed me, the full $6,500. Later I bought the piano on credit and borrowed money to finance the construction of the basement apartment.

As I read through my writing of 1994, I continued to be amazed by my walk down memory lane. This was far more than a series of coincidences. There was power in what I had written. My intentions had indeed become reality.

I knew if it worked for me, without ever re-reading the writing after the conference, imagine what could happen for people who read their life goals every day. I discovered that the written word has a great impact on our unconscious mind.

> **"Every moment of your life is infinitely creative and the universe is endlessly bountiful. Just put forth a clear enough request, and everything your heart desires comes to you."**
>
> Shakti Gawain, author

The importance of focus and patience

The great aspect of time is that there are the same 24 hours in each day for everyone.

Time does not discriminate against people of a particular gender, race, religion or age. In this area of life we are completely equal. Patience is a key component for focus to work properly in your life. After you decide what you want to have happen in your life, you will need to stay focused on the outcome you want to have. Focus is the product of concentrated thought and action. It's almost like a muscle that becomes stronger as you practice staying focused on a particular goal for longer periods of time. As you see results, even small ones, you will feel encouraged to stay on target for your bigger life goals.

Patience is an integral part of what allows focus to work in one's life. Webster's dictionary describes patience as calmly enduring and persevering to the end. By visualizing the outcome you want to have, you will be able to keep your dream alive through patience, focus, and perseverance. Impatience can make someone feel so uneasy and annoyed that they may choose to give up on their dream. Stay calm and know that good things come to those who wait, and most importantly, to those who take action.

"All things come to those who wait, provided they know what they are waiting for."
Woodrow Wilson, former President

The importance of feelings

We all have a dream because of how it will make us feel or what it can do for our lives. Discovering WHY you want what you want is an important step of the creation process.

If your goal doesn't motivate you on some level to feel good in some way, it is not likely to be a goal you will reach. If there is no passion behind why you want a particular thing, you will probably not take the steps necessary for it to happen. This is just basic human psychology.

"Hope is not a plan."
Anderson Cooper, CNN reporter

Hoping for your dreams is not going to make them happen. All plans actually start out as thoughts and grow from there. For instance, perhaps you're hungry and you think to yourself "I want to cook something." Your next thought might be, "what shall I cook?" Next you may think, "I need to look in the refrigerator to see what food I can cook." Then your mind reminds you to assemble cooking utensils. All of these thoughts occur in a mere second or two of real time. Plans for our life evolve the same way.

One thought leads to another, which leads to another, which ultimately leads to a viable solution or idea. But it all starts with that first thought.

"A thought is the precursor to all action."
Ralph Waldo Emerson, poet

Your dream must make you feel good and provide a payoff. The payoff is the "what's in it for me." Ultimately it will be the motivator for the actions you need to take to reach your goals. The key is to think about what you want. This process may take some time. It may take you days or weeks to decide how important a particular idea is to you. Be patient with yourself and be willing to consider possibilities outside your comfort zone.

"What would you attempt to do if you knew you could not fail?"
Robert Schuller, author

Don't be concerned if all the pieces of your dream come together slowly and at first you barely have a clue how to get started. Sometimes the information gathering stage of your dream takes some time and research in order to form a realistic plan. Carry a small notebook, or blank note cards with you at all times so you can record ideas that come to you. I keep a little folder in my car that has built in sides so nothing falls out. It holds the ideas I write on note cards or scraps of paper. That way I don't miss out on any great ideas I hear on the radio or ideas that come to me as I'm driving.

Most newer cell phones have a voice memo feature where you can leave your ideas and reminders. You can also leave yourself a message on your home answering machine or you can send yourself an email.

"When you think it, ink it."
Mark Victor Hansen, author

Actor Jim Carrey's story

Belief in itself will not get us to our goal. But belief combined with action will. In 1987 when Jim Carrey wrote out a fake check to himself for $10 million and dated it eight years in advance, he was unconsciously preparing himself for his success. When he wasn't busy, he would hold the fake check and visualize and affirm his future. Jim was obviously a realist. He knew his dream would take some time.

Jim Carrey's story is truly remarkable. He overcame huge obstacles to achieve his dream of becoming an international film star. His life changed forever when his father lost his job and his family ended up living in a van.

Jim Carrey quit school at age 16 so he could work to help support his family. What if he had a belief that he had to have an education? What if he believed he had to have connections in Hollywood to get to the top? He was willing to take risks and to believe in himself when there was no reason, as yet, to believe.

Jim Carrey was also willing to pay his dues and to work hard to achieve his dream. He didn't expect to go straight from working comedy clubs to a lead role in a film. He started out with bit parts in movies. He worked on a television show for several seasons, and then had a starring role in a film. It was a gradual process for him, just as it will be for you.

Despite the current situation, keep believing in yourself and your dreams.

Jim Carrey kept his eye on the future even when circumstances seemed dire. In 1987 he had a new baby and was working comedy clubs. He and his family were sleeping on a mattress on the floor. Jim Carrey believed it was all temporary and that he would eventually achieve huge success. This is an important key to his life story.

A reporter once asked Jim, "Come on, do you really believe you deserve $20 million a film?" He exclaimed, "Absolutely! I'm worth every penny!" Jim Carrey not only believed he was worth $20 million a film, he was willing to do whatever was necessary to achieve his dreams. He took acting lessons, hired an agent and manager, and studied his craft for hours on end.

Jim Carrey is a dedicated and constantly evolving performer. He is committed to improving his skills on every level in order to give his best performance. Jim Carrey exemplifies the value of constant self-improvement, the importance of never giving up, and a belief in one's self. I believe that someday he will win an Oscar for best actor.

***Jim Carrey is an Operation Smile donor.

"To accomplish great things, we must not only act, but also dream; not only plan, but also believe."
Anatole France, author

The story of a six year old writing his future

The Writing Your Future method is for people of all ages. In 1988 Tommy Tighe, age 6, wanted to sell a bumper sticker that would impact the world. It was scribbled in a child's handwriting and read:

Peace in the world. Do it for us kids, Please!
Tommy

Tommy Tighe illustrates beautifully the magic of asking for what you want. Here is his original goal list.

1. Call about cost (baseball card collateral)
Tommy called a private bank that loans money to children under age 18. He borrowed $454 to print 1,000 stickers.

2. Have bumper sticker printed

3. Make a plan to repay the loan
Originally he was selling bumper stickers for $1.50, later he doubled his price to $3.00!

4. Find out how to tell people
Tommy did research with the help of his parents.

5. Give a talk at school
This was a real confidence builder for him.

6. Get addresses of political leaders
He obtained them at the local library.

7. Write a letter to all the leaders of other countries and send them all a bumper sticker

He sent a bumper sticker and a bill to Soviet Union President Mikhail Gorbachev for $1.50. Mikhail sent the money and a signed picture of himself that said "Go for peace, Tommy!"

Tommy went to former US President Ronald Reagan's home and spoke to the gatekeeper about buying a bumper sticker for the president. He did.

8. Call the local newspaper

Marty Shaw, a journalist from the Orange County Register, asked Tommy if he could really have an impact on world peace. Tommy said. "I think you have to be eight or nine years old to stop all the wars in the world." The interview led to more media attention.

9. Talk to everyone about peace

In 1989, Joan Rivers asked Tommy on her television show if his bumper sticker could really cause peace in the world. A smiling Tommy said, "So far I've had it out two years and got the Berlin Wall down. I'm doing pretty good, don't you think?"

Notice how Tommy didn't have twenty or thirty items on his to-do list? Keep it to ten or less. If you make it too complicated the temptation is to give up before you see any results. Keep it simple.

What do you really want?

The first step in Writing Your Future is to think about what you want. For the moment, I would like you to suspend all disbelief about your future. Don't worry whether something seems realistic or not. In the beginning, everything you write will be just a possibility that comes to your mind. Possibilities are the "maybes" of your life. In the next few pages, I will show you how to change your life possibilities into goals. Until then just keep asking yourself, "What do I really want?" If there were no limits to your dreams, what would they be?

As you begin Writing Your Future, you might think of people who are doing what you would like to do, or who have things you would like to have. Some people find that looking through magazines at a book store or a library stimulates their imagination to discover what they want. You may also find that closing your eyes and visualizing in your mind helps you uncover how you really want your life to be. Through trial and error, you will discover the form of visualization that works best for you. The key is to practice it on a regular basis.

"You and I are essentially infinite choice-makers. In every moment of our existence, we are in that field of all possibilities where we have access to an infinity of choices."
Deepak Chopra, physician and author

You must believe you deserve whatever you want to achieve

This can be the most difficult part of the Writing Your Future process. It's important to believe that you deserve whatever it is you are trying to create in your life. It's important to shift your focus as soon as your mind starts thinking fearful and doubting thoughts, otherwise your unconscious mind can sabotage your success.

There have been several studies about lottery winners. Did you know that many of the winners are broke within five years? People shake their heads in amazement to discover this. How could anyone let millions of dollars slip through their hands? "It's easy," say the lottery winners who squandered their money. Some of the reasons they gave for losing the money include choosing bad investments, employing bad money managers, not getting enough information before investing, friends and strangers putting pressure on them to give them money and spending large sums of money on things they didn't need i.e. luxury automobiles and multiple homes.

Perhaps if a person does not feel worthy of their newfound wealth, their unconscious mind creates ways for them to get rid of the money they did not "deserve." They can then return to their former lifestyle, one in with which they are comfortable and familiar.

Why belief is so important

Anyone can have a dream but believing in the dream is an important aspect of making it come true. Webster's dictionary defines a belief as; a conviction that certain things are true. Believing something to be true requires an element of faith that it can eventually come true.

Belief is almost like a muscle that has to be exercised to grow. Your confidence and belief will develop as you complete even small steps toward your dream and begin to see results.

While you are Writing Your Future, you will want to eliminate the word "try" from your vocabulary. To "try" is a half-hearted attempt without conviction. If your dream is truly important in your life, you will endeavor to make it happen. If one way doesn't work, you will find another way. If that way doesn't succeed either, you will keep going until you find a way to bring your dream to fruition. This is why having a plan and being flexible are essential.

Action is one of the other building blocks for bringing dreams to reality, but first, you will need to decide what you want. As you spend time thinking about what you really desire for your life, you can write down ideas in the pages following the explanation of the seven suggested life areas.

So find a pencil, pen, or a computer, and let's begin Writing Your Future.

"Trying is failing with honor."
Dr. Michael Beckwith, teacher

Money and Possessions

This category would include anything that costs money such as travel, cars, houses, furniture, clothing and other possessions. It would include anything having to do with money management such as reducing and eliminating debt, creating savings accounts, IRA's, 401k's, learning about the stock market or investing in real estate. What kind of home would you live in? What kind of car would you like to drive?

Career and Education

Include anything you would need to do to advance your job or to get into a new profession: get more education for a job, negotiate a pay raise, obtain a higher paying job, learn extra skills for a new position, look for a new job, attend night school, have someone teach you a new skill, go to college, or finish a degree. What kind of hours would you work? How will you get to work each day? How long of a commute to work is acceptable to you?

Health, Fitness, and Appearance

Anything having to do with maintaining optimum health belongs here. Perhaps it would be eliminating or reducing junk food, maintaining your ideal weight, working out, drinking more water, learning or playing a sport, or committing to an exercise plan even if that means just walking every day.

Any changes to your physical appearance like hair color and haircut would belong in this category. What would your health and weight be like? What kinds of clothes and shoes would you like to wear?

Romance, Friends, and Family Life

Write down anything you would want in order to achieve more fun, unity, and love in your life. Include things like dinner with friends, date nights with a loved one, a cleaner house, more mutual respect, more help from the family, more organization, attending parties or having one at your home. What kind of person do you want to date or to marry? What kinds of characteristics would they have? What things would they value in their life? When you get together with friends or with a loved one, what kinds of things would you like to do? What would your friends be like?

Dreams and Aspirations

This category could include whatever long term dreams you have for your life that would take five years or more to achieve. Maybe you want to learn to play a musical instrument or learn another language. Would you like to run a marathon or hike Mt. Everest? Perhaps you want to renovate a large part of your home or office. Many of these goals take time because training, education, and research may need to be completed or money saved toward your goal.

Fun and Vacations

On this list include everything you would do for fun. List hobbies you want to explore like learning to paint or draw, gourmet cooking, renovating a car, wood working, or other hobbies. How will you spend your free time? Do you want to pursue a sport? Would you join a crafts club or a hiking club? What places in the world do you want to visit? Who do you want to go with? How much money will it cost to travel?

Spiritual and Contribution

Everything you would do to make a contribution to the world would be written here. Such things as: donating clothes or money to a charity, helping an elderly neighbor, picking up trash in the street, volunteering, organizing a community event, being on a committee to help your city, recycling, carpooling, or conserving energy. Perhaps you want to teach or volunteer at your place of worship, or at the local school. Include ways of giving help in your home by cooking, cleaning, and other household tasks.

It was discovered in studies of volunteers that they tend to live longer and stay healthier. There are so many ways to make a difference in the world. What legacy would you like to leave the world? Find a cause that interests you and make a commitment to stay involved, even if it's only a few times a year or once a month.

Possibilities for Money and Possessions

Possibilities for Career and Education

Possibilities for Health, Fitness, and Appearance

Possibilities for Love, Friends, and Family

Possibilities for Dreams and Aspirations

Possibilities for Fun and Vacations

Possibilities for Spirituality and Contribution

101 Things you want to do in your lifetime

As you go through your life, think of everything you want to BE, DO, or HAVE in your lifetime. It may take some time to decide what interests you. There is a 101 list at the back of this book for you to use. It's not important to write all 101 goals all at once.

Perhaps make an effort to review your list from time to time, such as the first Sunday of every month. You can add new goals as you think of them. Writing in pencil works well because many people find that as they review their list, their desires change.

As you go through your life, check off the goals you have completed and add a completion date next to the goal or you could write VICTORY and the date. You may also decide to delete an item or two as you think more about what you want to have in your future.

What are the top three things you want to BE, DO or HAVE within the next 6 months?

____

____

____

____

____

What are the top three things you want to BE, DO or HAVE in the next 2 years?

What are the top three things you want to BE, DO or HAVE in the next 3 - 5 years?

What are the top three things you want to BE, DO or HAVE in the next 5 - 10 years?

What are the top three things you want to BE, DO or HAVE in the next 10 - 15 years?

What are the top three things you want to BE, DO or HAVE in the next 15 - 20 years?

From a possibility to a defined goal

As you write ideas for your future, you may need a little time to think about your life possibilities. Once you have an idea of which possibilities you would like to change to goals, write them on Dream Cards.

Using Dream Cards

Dream Cards are 3x5 note cards on which you will write your dreams in the present tense, as if your wish is already occurring. You will be able to sort through your colored Dream Cards and easily see the area of your life that is most important to you. Create your own cards from colored paper or you can purchase them at our website:

www.writingyourfuture.com

It's important to write your goals in the present tense preferably with a descriptive word like happily, easily, etc. Invoking the "feeling" part of the goal is a key component. Most of us do things in life because of how it makes us feel. Feelings are the fuel of human behavior. At first you might want to write in pencil on the Dream Cards. Once you are sure you want the goal, re-write the Dream Card with a big marker pen.

"Cherish your vision and your dreams as they are the children of your soul; the blueprints of your ultimate achievements."

Napoleon Hill, author

There is power in the written word, especially when you start your writing with "I AM."

I am enjoying my higher paying job.
I am easily graduating from college on time.
I am enjoying my new relationship.
I am so happy to be driving my new car.

People who used Dream Cards to achieve goals

Mark Victor Hansen and Jack Canfield are co-authors of the multi-million selling *Chicken Soup for the Soul* series. Both men made a habit of writing their goals on note cards and reading them in the morning and at night. Mark wrote this sentence on a card, carried it with him, and read it several times a day.

I am so happy to be selling 1.5 million copies of Chicken Soup for the Soul by December 30, 1994.
They sold 1.3 million copies by that date.

How to effectively use your Dream Cards.

Write a one sentence, specifically worded dream in the present tense as if it is already happening.

Something like this:

I am so happy living in a sunny, modern home.
I am enjoying time with my hiking club.
I am so happy to be playing tennis once a week.

"A goal is merely a wish until it's written down."
Bill Maher, Life coach

3 steps for reading your Dream Cards

- Repeat the words of your Dream Card in your mind or say them out loud.
- See yourself doing or having your dream.
- Feel the feelings you would feel if your dream came true.

Importance of making your goals specific

SPECIFIC: I am increasing my income by ____ in the next six months (calculate the exact number).

VAGUE: I am making more money.

SPECIFIC: I am studying every night between 7 - 8 pm

VAGUE: I am studying harder everyday.

SPECIFIC: I am enjoying my new relationship with a person who is intelligent, affectionate, and fun.

VAGUE: I am enjoying my new relationship.

Money and Possessions (Green cards)

I am happily driving my silver 2003 VW Passat.
I am enjoying my new black leather couch.
I am saving ______ a month for my dream of _____.

Health, fitness, appearance (Blue cards)

I'm feeling healthy and full of life at _____lbs.
I'm so happy that my cholesterol is down ____ points.
It feels great to be running for 1 hour 3 days a week.

Career and Education (Orange cards)

I'm so happy my new job is within10 miles from home.
I am so happy to be receiving a pay raise by___.
I am happy to be finishing my classes by___.

Love, Friends, Family (Pink cards)

I'm so happy to be dating a fun, caring person by___.
I enjoy having my friends over every Friday night.
I am helping my family clean house every Sat. morning.

Hopes and Dreams (Yellow cards)

I am starting a skydiving class by ___.
I am excited to be going to Yosemite Park by____.
I am starting a home-based business by ____.

Fun and Vacations (Purple cards)

I enjoy meeting my friends for coffee every Friday night.
I am so happy to be going on a camping trip every ____.
I enjoy being on a soccer team.

Spiritual and Giving back (White cards)

I am so happy to be coaching little league by_____.
I enjoy helping at the homeless shelter once a month.
I'm so happy to be going on a retreat every year.

Using a Life Box

A Life Box is a box that contains things that remind you of happy and successful times.

You can put photos, emails, or cards that have a positive message in this box. By reading through cards and emails, you will recall that you are appreciated and loved. You might even want to create a tape of uplifting voicemails from friends, family, and bosses. You can play the tape whenever you are feeling discouraged or unmotivated.

The Life Box is also the place to put note cards on which you can write past goals you have achieved. Simply write what goal you achieved and write the word VICTORY across the card. These Victory Cards will remind you of what you accomplished in the past and serve as encouragement for you to take action on your future goals. You may even one to put several of the Victory Cards on your Dream Board.

It's easy to allow a bad experience or a series of setbacks to derail your dreams for days, weeks, months, and even years. Using a Life Box will boost your confidence and remind you that you are a valuable human being. On days when you are feeling down and not motivated to write or think about your goals, you can go through your Life Box to get re-inspired.

"Encouragement is the oxygen of the soul."
Anonymous

Using a Dream Board

A Dream Board is a visual representation of your life goals. A Dream Board is a cork bulletin board, dry erase board, or a piece of cardboard that will hold photos, drawings, copies of checks, magazine clippings or whatever you wish to put on it. For best results, I recommend that you place a Dream Card near each photo or magazine clipping you place on the Dream Board.

You may want to consider putting a photo on your computer using the "wallpaper" feature. Your dream will then be on the background of your visual field for many hours a day.

If you are a very private person and you don't want your friends, family, or roommates to see your Dream Board, then use a Dream Book. It's important to make a habit of looking through your Dream Book often, preferably every day. If you are using a Dream Board, place it in an area where you will walk by several times a day so your mind can easily record your vision.

Many people create a Writing Your Future journal to write about their dreams as if they are already occurring. Even if you write in your journal only once a month, you will find that it has great impact on your unconscious mind and it can assist you in bringing your goals to fruition.

"If you don't have a plan, you will find yourself working for someone who does."
W. Clement Stone, publisher, entrepreneur

One Man's Dream Board Success Story

In 1995, John Assaraf created a Dream Board and put it up on the wall in his home office. Whenever he saw something he wanted or a trip he wanted to take, he'd cut out a photo from a magazine depicting something similar and glue it to the board. Then he'd close his eyes and visualize himself already enjoying the object of his desire.

In May 2000, having just moved into his new California home from the state of Indiana, he and his 5 year old son opened one of the boxes that had been in storage four years. On one of the many Dream Boards was a picture of the house John had just purchased. He was stunned. It wasn't just a picture of a similar house, it was HIS house, a 7,000 square foot home with an office complex and a tennis court that he had cut out of a California Dream Homes magazine four years before!

In case you think it can't happen to you, John Assaraf was a 9th grade dropout. He attributes his early success to spending time in the sauna of a local club so he could listen to the businessmen talk. He is well known in business circles for his innovative approaches to building new companies.

***This story is from the documentary style movie "The Secret."

Another Dream Board success story

I put the headline of the local newspaper on my Dream Board. I set a goal to call them about writing an article about this book. Two months later I was working on this book at a coffeehouse and a reporter from that same newspaper approached me. He was doing a story about people who did some of their work in coffeehouses and wanted to interview me. He even took pictures of me and this book. Every day I focused on the newspaper caption on my Dream Board and it happened!

Katherine Woodward Thomas, author of "Calling in the One, Seven Weeks to Attract the Love of your Life" tells her true story. Read how she wrote her future.

Written February 22, 1999

My dream is to be a writer of significance—to write books which exalt and edify the human spirit. I see a book out in bookstores around the country having a life of its own.

Also, by my birthday (August), I see a beautiful engagement ring on my finger. It is reflecting a deep rooted love between my husband to be and myself. He is my perfect mate. I like myself when I am with him. I feel supported and nurtured by our relationship. I feel protected by him—loved, respected, held up—I love and am loved deeply and completely. I see this. I also see being pregnant with my husband's baby.

On the surface this seems like a ridiculous fantasy. Why? At the time of this writing (almost March), Katherine did not have any men in her life. How would she be engaged in five months?

The other problem was that she was almost 42 years old. Any doctor would tell you her odds of becoming pregnant without laboratory intervention would be slim. The part she wrote about having a book out in the bookstores? She had never written a book.

Some would call this whole writing exercise a delusion, unless they knew the power of Writing Your Future. Here's what transpired after Katherine wrote this diary entry.

"When I reread this diary entry two years later I did a double take. I checked out the date at least three times before I finally believed that I'd written it a full SIX weeks before I met Mark for the third time. (They had dated previously). It sounded so much like my real life, that I was stunned. At the time, I was 41 and childless, and I'd never had a book deal. I ended up having my first child, a baby girl, at age 43. That's the power of standing inside a vision."

"Writing creates beliefs
beliefs create attitudes
attitudes create feelings
feelings determine actions
actions create results."
Shad Helmstetter, author

Creating a Dream Jar

A Dream Jar holds a visual representation of your goal. For instance, let's say you want to go to Paris, France. You could tape a picture of the Eiffel tower on the Dream Jar and then put money inside that you save toward your dream. Some of the money you put in your Dream Jar could come by not using money on a usual expenditure e.g. eating out, specialty coffees, cigarettes, alcohol or clothes.

You will notice that you will begin to look forward to the wonderful feeling you get when you deposit money in your Dream Jar. Inside the jar you can put money, deposit slips, and perhaps a running tally of the money saved in your Dream account. Each time you deposit money in your Dream Jar, you are one step closer to your goal.

It's important to deposit the money from your jar into your designated savings account every week or two. If your money is too accessible to you or other family members, it will be easy to use the money for other things. You may want to set up different savings accounts at a local bank for different dreams. You will discover that through disciplined planning and saving, you will eventually achieve your dreams.

"The very best thing you can do for the whole world is to make the most of yourself."
Wallace Wattles, author

To maximize your success, you will want to assemble the following items:

1. Pencil, pen, black marker
2. Dream Cards: 3 x 5 note cards
   in seven different colors if possible
3. Writing Your Future journal
4. Dream Board, Dream Book, or Dream Jar
5. Large Life Box container

You can write your goals on plain white note cards. However, I believe that colored cards work better. Color has been shown to affect our brain in a positive way. You can either make your own or buy them on our website.

Green	Money and Possessions
Orange	Career and Education
Blue	Health and Fitness
Pink	Love and Family Life
Yellow	Dreams and Aspirations
Purple	Fun and Vacations
White	Spiritual and Contribution

> **"Your subconscious mind never wanders. It always pays attention. It is always ready to make happen in your life those things positive and negative that you are imagining."**
> Leland Cooley, author

What to write, When to write

- Start writing with the end in mind.
- See yourself with the object of your desire, and doing whatever it is you want to do.
- Feel the feelings you would have if you obtained your wish.

When you read your Dream Cards, pause for 3-10 seconds or so between each card and feel the feeling you would feel if you achieved your dream.

At this point, you might not have any idea of how to achieve your goal. That is not important at this time. As you think about what you want, bit by bit, your mind will lead you to the pieces of information needed to help you reach your goals.

Write in a place where you can be without distractions for 5-10 minutes. You want to be in a believing and excited frame of mind. If necessary, get up early to do your writing before other members of your household awaken, or stay up later in the evening.

If you live in a busy household and people are constantly curious about what you're doing, write in the bathroom if necessary. Perhaps prepare a bubble bath and do some writing in the bathtub.

"You'll see it when you believe it."
Dr. Wayne Dyer, author

W. Clement Stone, a multi-millionaire publisher, used to spend an hour every morning in the bathtub writing and dreaming. He credits this time as an essential part of his day. Writing Your Future will only take a few minutes and it will help you achieve your dreams more quickly.

Write it as if it's already happening

According to recent studies, our mind can not distinguish between a believing, imagined thought with feeling and the real event. There is enormous power in how we speak and in the words we use. It is important to state your goals with "I am" rather than "I will." When you write "I will" it leaves some doubt whether you will actually be taking action.

It's also important to write your goal in the present tense with a future date. It could be one month, one year, three years, five, ten, or even twenty years out. It's important to believe whatever you are writing is truly possible. There is tremendous power in a vivid imagination and in stating your goals in "I am" form.

Example: *I am so happy to be driving my 2005 Silver Passat with a sunroof by* ______________.

Tip: DON'T write your affirmations in a negative way. i.e.; "I no longer waste time on the weekends."

Your mind hears "waste time on weekends." Always state a goal in a positive way so that you have a greater chance of success.

Example. *"I easily make good use of my time on the weekends."*

Using end dates for your goals

Being as specific as possible will increase your chances of your dream happening. Avoid the use of writing the word "someday," like "someday I am going to visit ____". Someday could be fifty years away. Our goals are most effective with an end date. If you are concerned about setting a timeline that is too soon, make it an extra year out. Some people feel incredible pressure after setting dates for their goals and others need dates in order to motivate them. Whether or not you put dates on your Dream Cards, the most important step is to take action on a consistent basis.

I am graduating from college by____.
I am applying for a new job by____.
I am so happy to own my first home by____.

I easily run for 20 minutes a day.
I easily drink six glasses of water each day.
It feels good to read my Dream Cards every day.

You will have the greatest chance for fulfillment of your life dreams if you read your Dream Cards immediately upon awakening and before you go to sleep. Your unconscious mind is more accessible at those times. Remember to pause between reading each Dream Card and visualize with feeling what it would be like to have your dream come true.

"It's time to start living the life you've imagined."
Henry James, author

Roma Downey is the spokesperson for Operation Smile, a charity that corrects the facial deformities of children. For nine seasons, she played an angel on the hit show "Touched by an Angel." Here is Roma's story about writing her future.

I had been reading a pictorial essay in a magazine. It showed the interior of a beach home of an actor friend of mine. I just loved the look and the feel of his home. I pulled out the pages from the magazine and put them in an envelope and I attached a note. I wrote with all the confidence I could muster, "One day I shall have a Malibu beach house." I sealed the envelope, put it in a drawer and promptly forgot about it.

Years later I was visiting Malibu, California and contemplating buying a house. After viewing the house that afternoon, I went back to Salt Lake City. I was on the phone with my business manager, who said, "If you're interested in buying, you need to make an offer because there is another interested party."

That night, I needed to write something down and I opened the drawer of my desk and it stuck. I gave the drawer a strong pull and an envelope ricocheted out from the back of the drawer. I saw the photos and the note attached and instantly remembered. Of course, I called my manager and submitted an offer. I now live in a Malibu beach house just as I had written.

Tip: Read biographies of inspirational people. They are about ordinary people doing extraordinary things and there is hope in them for all of us.

The power of music while you write

Music has been proven to release endorphins in the brain. Writing is easier for many people while listening to certain types of music, especially instrumental music. This kind of music is wonderful because there are no words to distract the listener. It's easy to research different kinds of music on the internet that will stimulate your creativity. It's also productive to play music from your past that evokes memories of happy, peaceful and prosperous times.

Baroque music slows the heart rate to around sixty beats per minute which allows your creative thoughts to flow more easily. The string quartet music of Johann Sebastian Bach is wonderful background music while you are writing. Consider exploring other types of Baroque music as well.

Just as some people like to write and dream in noisy coffeehouses, there are many people who need complete silence to have creativity surge in their souls. Other people write best when they are out in nature or in an uncluttered environment. Find that place where you feel free to open up your mind to exploring what you would like to have happen in your life. Music can be a great tool to assist you in putting your feelings and dreams into a written form.

"Music is an elixir for the soul."
Anonymous

Your unconscious mind takes things literally. It's important that you do not verbalize or write down negative outcomes to your dreams. Your mind can actually create events according to your beliefs as illustrated with the following story.

I had a friend years ago who constantly talked about and often emailed me his "easy come, easy go" philosophy about money. He earned a lot of money but there was always something that "just happened" in his life that cost him large amounts of money. My friend had a serious accident in a foreign country. At that time, some insurance companies didn't cover medical expenses that occurred outside the United States. He was left with a huge medical bill that took him years to pay off. He believed money came easily and "left" easily. Perhaps on some kind of unconscious level, he attracted yet another situation for his money to "go".

Nearly every one of us struggles from time to time with negative thoughts or ways we might co-create our future through focusing on what can go wrong. Obviously, life isn't perfect, and random good and bad events can happen. But why invite those occurrences into our lives by thinking and speaking negatively?

> **"The brain simply believes what you tell it most. What you tell it about yourself, it will create. It has no choice."**
>
> Shad Helmstetter, author

How a 77 year old man achieved his dream

My father had a dream of owning a second home in Florida. He wanted to buy his older brother's condo in a small beach town so he had his brother sign a first right of refusal to purchase the property. Every year he visited his brother he would walk the beach saying to himself, "someday I will be on this beach every day." He became acquainted with the town and his brother's neighbors, even telling them he would be living there someday! Eleven years after my dad formulated his desire, he signed papers to officially purchase the condo. My father credits writing his future, belief, and visualization as the keys to his dream coming true.

A 17 year old's story of obtaining a scholarship

"My goal was to obtain a scholarship to college. Even though I had been home schooled for most of my education, I still believed that with extra study and good grades, I could compete with other students. I spent a lot of time writing my college application essay. I labored over every word and asked for feedback from others before sending in my application and essay well in advance of each school's deadline that I had written on the calendar. Each morning I lay in my bed and pictured myself opening scholarship offers from the seven colleges I had applied to.
It's amazing how the extra time spent writing the college essay and visualizing has paid off. I am now in the process of deciding which of the five scholarship offers I would like to accept."

Believe you deserve to have what you want to create

Writing Your Future will not work to its full potential unless you believe that you deserve abundance. Having constant doubting and fearful thoughts can hinder or delay your goal coming to fruition. Affirmations do not work unless they are followed up with belief and action.

It's not always easy, but it all starts with an intention to be positive and eventually negative thoughts will just not come to your mind as often. Many people struggle with feelings of negativity, pessimism, or even unworthiness. They can be having thoughts like any of the following:

I tried that before and it didn't work.
My (family, parents, bosses) won't let me do that.
People will think I'm stupid/crazy for going for a dream like that.

I can't deal with uncertainty. I'll just stick with what I'm doing. At least I know what to expect.
I could never imagine myself doing that.

I don't deserve _____. It wouldn't feel right.
I never get what I want.

It is important to realign your thinking as soon as you think anything negative. Don't allow those thoughts to take root in your mind. As soon as you think a negative thought say to yourself: *Delete that!*

I do deserve for____to happen.
I can accomplish ____ with a plan of action.
I am open to receiving help to achieve my goals.
I am open and worthy of increasing my income.
I have enough time and money for my dreams.

Recall people who you know personally, or people you have heard of, whose lives are abundant and happy. Then say to yourself:

Prosperity happens to millions of people every day and I believe it can happen for me.

Limiting thoughts like, "I can't afford it" have no business in your mind. Adjust that thought to, "HOW can I afford it?" Then write down possibilities for bringing in more money to achieve your dream. At first, you may not be able to think of how to bring in more money. But if you did know, what do you think could be sources of money? Be open and willing to consider many different kinds of possibilities.

You can change your thoughts by adjusting what you believe is truly possible for your life. But it will take a concerted effort to change your negative thoughts to positive ones. When a negative, doubting thought comes to your mind, envision yourself hitting a DELETE button.

"Affirmations will not work until we change our thoughts."
Louise Hay, publisher and author

What is a mastermind group?

A mastermind group is a small number of people who support and give ideas to each other to help achieve goals. The purpose of the group is to help each individual be the best they can be in business and in life. The focus of these groups is on the future rather than the past. This can be a great way to stay on target with your goals and to get creative input from others.

Mastermind groups work best with 4-10 people. Some groups meet only once a month, some every week. Many of these groups start the session with an inspirational story and then check in with each member of the group.

It works best to set limits on how long each person can speak. It's also important to start and end at the times that are designated, otherwise people may quit the group.

With the internet, it's easy to find mastermind groups online. Most groups meet in person, but some work through emailing. Not all input or advice received will be good. Use discernment and listen to your "inner voice." If you are given negative input, don't allow it to linger in your mind. It will only slow your progress and leave you feeling fearful, doubtful, and nervous.

> **"The best way to get everything you want, is to help others achieve everything they want."**
>
> Zig Ziglar, speaker

The mastermind group is a great place to ask others if they know anyone outside the group that could help you with your dream. Talk to people who have succeeded at what you want to do. It's important to always seek wise counsel. Many entrepreneurs invest in business or life coaches. Do not attempt to do it all alone. That's a recipe for potential failure and can result in feelings of defeat.

Who to share your dreams with

It is best to share your dreams with people who will support and uplift you. Limit your time, and if possible, disassociate yourself from people who have constant negative input.
They say things like:

You're not being realistic.
You don't have the education.
You don't have the right connections.
You don't have the money to do that.
No one in your family has ever______.

That sounds too hard to do.
Don't waste your time. It won't happen.
How are you going to do all that?
You'll just be disappointed.
You could never get an appointment to see____.
I don't want to have to say "I told you so."

> **"Argue for your limitations, and sure enough they are yours."**
> Richard Bach, author

Negative people may also cite statistics which state that 95% of all small businesses fail in the first three years, and other words of doom. If Bill Gates had listened to talk like this, he never would have founded Microsoft. It takes courage to dream big. Be open to positive suggestions, but use good judgment whether or not you incorporate the ideas into your plan.

There are many reasons why people may try to discourage someone's dreams. Perhaps they get a feeling of superiority by putting others down. Maybe they are envious of your courage. If you succeed with your goal, it might make them feel like they should be doing more with their lives. Perhaps they had been hurt by their own failures in life and feel it's their duty to warn you to not expect too much. It could also be something as simple as that particular person's own inner negativity coming out.

"Feed back is the breakfast of champions."
Ken Blanchard and Spencer Johnson, authors

Part Three
What to do about fear and worry

There are going to be times when Writing Your Future feels strange, unrealistic, and you might be tempted to stop writing and reading your Dream Cards. You may be worried that the things you are writing about can't possibly come true. Perhaps you are bombarded with thoughts like these:

I don't know anyone to seek advice from.
It costs money to get my idea going.
What if I put a lot of time and money into my dream and it fails?

Fear is an acronym for Fantasized Experiences Appearing Real.

Learning from other people's experiences

Whenever you are trying out something new, it's beneficial to talk to others about whatever it is you are attempting to do. One brief conversation with someone could save you thousands of dollars or months and years of trying something that might not work like you think it could. Be open, and be willing to listen and to learn.

"I've lived a long life and had many miseries, most of which never happened."
Mark Twain, author

Dealing with memories of past failures

It's important to rid ourselves of negative thoughts about past events and fear thoughts about possible negative scenarios that could take place in the future. You may be bombarded by recurring thoughts like these:

I tried that before and it didn't work.
You can't teach an old dog new tricks.
There's no way I could ever___because___.
_____said I could never do that.
It's hopeless, I could never do_____.

These are limiting statements that are detrimental to your dreams as well as your peace of mind. If your mind starts visualizing a negative outcome to your dreams, immediately replace it with something like:

Delete that; how it could turn out is_____.
Delete that; I can do ____, I just need more information.

If you make a mistake, or you've said the wrong thing today, say to yourself:

I am capable of doing better than that.
Next time I will_____.

If you owe someone an apology or an explanation, give it immediately so you don't spend precious life energy on regrets.

Our thoughts about our life are very powerful. Do not let a negative story play out in your mind. Refrain from repeatedly talking about your fears with someone or writing about possible negative outcomes. Think, speak, and write with positive words.

There is a lot of power in forgetting and forgiving. If we have truly forgiven, we will also have forgotten many of our past unpleasant moments. Some people easily forgive others, but have a difficult time forgiving themselves. Here are some phrases you can say to yourself:

I'm no longer like that. I'm a different person now;
I now do____when in that situation.
I wasn't myself at the time I_____.
I made a poor choice. I know I won't do that again.
I now keep my promises and commitments.
I did/said the wrong thing, but I made, or am making amends.

I forgive myself, or I am in the process of forgiving myself.

Making mistakes is part of the human experience. We've all said or done things that we wish we hadn't. After you have done what you can to make amends, you must let it go. Unforgiveness will only drain your life's energy and keep you from achieving your dreams.

"The past does not equal the future."
Tony Robbins, motivational speaker

10 steps to reduce worry so you can write again

1. Get information. Most of what we worry about is not accurate and is exaggerated.

2. Eat right and drink water for proper brain maintenance. Exercise even if it's only a fast walk for ten minutes. The key is to get your heart rate up.

3. Give and receive hugs and kind words. Be an encourager. The best way to get out of being stuck is to reach out and help someone else.

4. Never worry alone: talk to a friend, counselor, spouse or relative. Caution: Seek a solution or a new way of handling a situation. Re-telling the same story will only keep you feeling stuck.

5. Stay positive despite the current situation. Don't allow your mind to run wild. Remember FEAR is Fantasized Experiences Appearing Real.

6. Limit the time spent watching and reading the news; much of it can be depressing and negative. If there is something important happening in the world, you will find out about it.

7. Avoid contact with people who are negative, complaining, and draining most of the time. Try to spend time with positive people that you can learn from.

8. Get enough sleep at night. During the day take some time to calm your mind, even if it is for 2-15 minutes. Take slow, deep breaths and ask yourself, "What is it I need to know about how to achieve my goal?"

9. Give to others first and reap the rewards later. Remember, "What goes around, comes around."

10. Cultivate an attitude of gratitude. Even when there are challenges in life there are always things to appreciate i.e. the kindness of a stranger, family, good health, clothes, running water, enough food, shelter or access to transportation.

Cultivating a spirit of gratitude

It's been said that a person can't be unhappy and grateful at the same time. I found that by using a Gratitude Log my life immediately felt richer and happier. I use an 8x11 sheet of paper and I make 14 lines across the paper so I can write something everyday for two weeks. The best part is that it takes only 10-30 seconds to write something positive that happened.

Some days nothing special will happen until early afternoon or evening. Some days many things will transpire. Even if something mundane happened like finding money in the street, write it down. You could also write something like a friend called, or you received a nice card or email. It doesn't have to be a significant event. I believe that the Gratitude Log works because the unconscious mind is looking for something good to report and that attracts wonderful occurrences to us.

Consider creating a Gratitude Life List of 101 things you are grateful for in your life. You can keep adding to it with significant events from your daily gratitude log or you can add to it as you recall events from your past for which you are especially grateful. I keep my Gratitude Logs in a large envelope in my Life Box.

Tip: Around Jan 1st open your envelope of Gratitude Logs and read through the 365 wonderful things that happened in your life during the previous year.

The power of language

You have probably heard the cliché, "It's not what you say but how you say it." It's important to write out what you will say before meeting with an important contact. If you don't want to write out sample dialogue, write out key words you plan to use. Because you will have practiced, key phrases you have written down will be on the tip of your tongue.

Preparation for a phone call or a meeting is extremely important. You might even practice your presentation wearing the clothes you will be wearing at the time of the meeting. Perhaps use a tape recorder or video camera so you can make corrections to your delivery. Consider practicing your presentation with someone who is open to giving you feedback. You can then work out any stumbling blocks before you talk to the actual person you intend to meet with. Be open to the words that you are asked to adjust. After receiving feed back, rewrite your script or key points, and then practice again.

Use good judgment about whether to act on all suggestions that are given to you. After you make adjustments, call or get in front of your intended audience. After your presentation, be sure to give the person you are speaking with time to respond. You already know what you are going to say. The person in front of you is hearing it for the first time.

"Alone we can do little, together we can do so much."
Helen Keller, blind-deaf-mute

Visualize a positive outcome to your meeting or phone conversation. It's also good to do a little research on the internet about the person you intend to meet. Perhaps speak with some of their colleagues. You might consider beginning your conversation by giving a sincere compliment or a comment about one of their interests. Everyone likes to hear how they impacted the lives of others. These compliments must be your true feelings or your recipient will immediately sense a hidden agenda. Always be sincere.

If you ask someone for a couple of minutes or a specific time to meet, clarify how much time they are willing to give to hear your proposal, then honor the time you asked for. The person you are speaking with can always choose to extend the conversation if they want to.

Studies show that on average, 60% of all business is sold after five attempts with the same person, yet 40% of salespeople give up after the first attempt! If the person you met was abrupt or cold, consider that they may been having a bad day. Make contact again a week or two later before you give up.

Bombarding people with emails, phone calls, and personal notes can result in someone choosing not to do business with you. Perhaps limit your contact to bimonthly, monthly, or quarterly. Be professional and considerate.

**"Ask as if you expect to get it.
Ask from someone who
can give it to you."**
Jack Canfield, author

Don't give up after you have given a well prepared presentation. Perhaps the time isn't right for the person or company you want to do business with. It's important to stay in touch and perhaps the seed you planted will eventually take root.

Today there are so few people who take the time to handwrite and mail thank you cards. Your sincerity and follow-up will make you stand out in the crowd. It could be something as simple as this:

Thank you for taking the time to speak with me the other day. I've enclosed a card so if your company's plans change, you will know how to reach me.

Thank you for meeting with me the other day. If you think of someone who might use my service, please contact me with their name and number and I will follow up immediately.

*Thank you for spending time with me the other day.
I appreciate your kindness and your input.*

Thank you for taking time to speak with me by phone the other day. I look forward to working with you regarding_____.

"People will forget what you say, they will forget what you do, but they never will forget how you make them feel."
Maya Angelou, author

Celebrating past achievements

Make a list of all the things you have accomplished in the past. Write each of them on a separate Dream Card with the corresponding color from the 7 life areas. Write VICTORY across the cards and put them in your Life Box. As you reflect back on your life, it may take some time to write all the things you have accomplished. It doesn't have to be something significant. It can be something for which you are proud i.e. keeping a promise, exercising every day, turning in a project on time, or helping the less fortunate. By doing this, you will be celebrating what you achieved in the past.

Victory Cards will serve as encouragement and proof that you have completed many things in the past, and the future holds wonderful things for you as well. For most people, what they've accomplished in the past, they did without written goals. Imagine what you can accomplish in your life with focused attention on your dreams.

People tend to remember and dwell on the things in their life that didn't happen the way they wanted much more than their successes. If you practice Writing Your Future, you will soon notice that you will eventually train your mind to sort for the positives. You may also notice how you feel happier and more grateful for your life experiences.

> **"The greatest mistake you can make in life is to continually be afraid you will make one."**
> Elbert Hubbard, writer

Five ways to improve your mood in 15 minutes

It's difficult to do any part of the Writing Your Future method when you are in a low mood and feeling unconvinced, overwhelmed or unmotivated.

1. Read through your Life Box of past successes and cards from friends.
2. Call an encouraging friend or mentor.
3. Give yourself positive self talk like, "Tomorrow is another day," or "I can do this; I just need more information."
4. Go for a 10 minute fast walk.
5. Clean out a junk drawer, a small closet or organize your desk.

Setting a timer is a great way to stay focused for a short period of time. Spending just five to fifteen minutes de-cluttering a surface area, or Writing Your Future can boost your confidence in your ability to tackle the larger goals of your life. You will also notice how much better you feel when you have taken the steps to improve your living space and "inner space."

When Thomas Edison would become stuck when working on an invention, he would take a cat nap and more often than not, his assistants say Edison would wake up and exclaim, "I have the answer!" Obviously, the answer doesn't always pop up that quickly, but sometimes it does. Keep paper and a pen or pencil near you at all times so when a thought comes to you about a step you can take toward your dream you will be ready to write it down.

Other ways to reduce feeling overwhelmed

Our unconscious mind is very powerful. Get rid of clothes and objects that remind you of unhappy or traumatic times. We wear 10% of our clothes 90% of the time. If you haven't worn some clothes in years, sell them, trade them, give them away and feel your energy soar. Make room in your life for new possessions to come into your life.

Don't keep things around that remind you of a failed relationship or business. You may not consciously remember the upsetting events that transpired, but your unconscious mind may. Do not live in the past. Stay in the present moment and you will find yourself feeling lighter and happier.

At times I have had a hard time giving away clothes I haven't worn for a long time. My rationale used to be that I couldn't give away all those clothes because I had paid so much money for them and I might wear them again someday. Eventually I realized that they were just taking up space in my closet and I didn't feel good wearing those clothes anymore. Even looking at them in the closet became an energy drain because my intuition kept reminding me to give them away. I eventually gave away bags and bags of clothes to a local charity and two weeks later, a girlfriend gave me hundreds of dollars worth of expensive evening gowns and business attire.

"Unless we think of others and do something for them, we miss one of the greatest sources of happiness."

Ray Lyman Wilbur, physician

Deciding what to complete

Many of us get discouraged by things that are incomplete in our life. Every time your mind sees something that is unfinished it takes a little bit of your life energy. When you are bogged down by too many incomplete actions in your life, it makes it more difficult to have sufficient energy to achieve your dreams. For instance, perhaps you have weeds in your yard that need to be removed. You may think to yourself, "That looks bad. I wish someone would do something about it." Perhaps it doesn't bother others in your family. But if you are irritated by it, then put it on your list of things to complete.

Sometimes the bigger projects take valuable time that you may not have. Not every project is worth completing and some may need to be discarded. Give yourself permission to remove it from your "to do list." Perhaps you've had a misunderstanding and you owe someone an explanation or an apology. Maybe you need to thank someone for something they have done for you. Once you have the conversation, write the letter, or send the email you will be amazed at how much better you feel. If you owe someone money, contact them and make a plan for repayment. The person to whom you owe money may also be drained on some level by the lack of a plan for repayment. You will notice that by completing the incompletes in your life you will actually gain energy that you can put toward your new life goals.

What to do when you find yourself feeling stuck

It's important to be aware of the issues that could cause many of us to give up on writing, and, ultimately, our dreams. If you are feeling overwhelmed by continual negative, doubting thoughts, consider balancing your brain chemistry. Money, success, a high IQ, and even a great family life will not solve the brain chemistry problem. It can be set off by a genetic predisposition, a stressful situation, or a traumatic event. Therapy and positive thinking techniques will not work to their full potential if you are experiencing unhealthy brain chemistry.

Harvard University conducted a double-blind study using fish oil for treatment resistant bi-polar and depressed patients, described in the book *The Omega 3 Factor* by Dr. Andrew Stoll. The results of the study were phenomenal. All of the patients on the fish oil felt significantly better immediately. There is also scientific evidence that not drinking enough water and not eating the right balance of carbohydrates and proteins can affect your brain and your emotions. *The Zone Diet* by Dr. Barry Spears is a great one to follow. Whatever food combining method you choose, a balanced approach to eating and drinking will keep you on target for feeling your best and for having energy to pursue your dreams.

"If you worried about falling off the bike, you'd never get on."
Lance Armstrong, athlete

How to deal with low moods that hinder your writing

Moods can be influenced by upsetting interactions with people, hormonal changes, low energy, low blood sugar, or lack of sleep. Know that they are just moods and they will pass. Time always seems to move so slowly when we are experiencing a crisis or a low mood. Acknowledge that you are in a low mood and say to yourself, "This too, shall pass." Consider taking a few minutes to go on a quick walk before you respond to a crisis and perhaps say or email something you might regret.

Often we just need more information to get beyond feeling stuck. Avoid talking about your low mood to others unless you are seeking solutions rather than just retelling the story. This is the time to affirm, "Everything I need to know will come to me in time," as well as other positive phrases.

It's amazing how a good meal, a good night's sleep, or a pep talk from a friend can make such a huge difference in our perception of a problem. The challenge in itself may not change, but sometimes a little distance and a more positive approach can make all the difference. Our unconscious mind can work out many of life's details during our sleep, so believe!

> **"I'll think about it tomorrow,**
> **because tomorrow is another day."**
> Scarlett O'Hara, Gone with the Wind

Do's and Don'ts of Writing Your Future

Do not write when you are in a low mood. This is the time to read your past success cards (Victory Cards) and to review emails and positive cards from your Life Box. It's also a good time to clean out your closets, refrigerator, or even a garage. As you do these mundane organizing tasks, you will discover that it opens up the space for new things and new ideas to come into your life.

Many people notice that ideas come to them when they are out in nature. If you like to hike, carry a small note book with you to capture ideas. Other people feel their creativity surge when they are in the shower, or in a lake or ocean. Studies show that the negative ions released by showerheads, waterfalls, and fountains have a positive effect on the brain.
I have one friend who spends a lot of time brainstorming in the shower. He has a waterproof board in his shower so he can to jot down ideas.

An encouraging word from a friend, family, or a mastermind group can be all it takes to move us from a low mood back into a believing frame of mind. Sometimes our negative tired energy works to block new ideas and possible solutions from coming to us. Believe things will improve and that the solution will come to you when you are in a better frame of mind.

"Worry is negative goal setting."
Lou Tice, motivational speaker

The Power of Taking Action

Twice in my life I have purchased homes in neighborhoods that were rundown. Each time, I had a similar experience. As soon as I started improving my home, other people in the neighborhood started fixing up their homes as well. Perhaps it took that first person to start the energy/movement of rehabilitation.

Within the next five years, 25 of the 30 homes on the block were repainted, remodeled, or re-landscaped. Another interesting part of this story is that none of the work I was doing was visible to others. I was only doing interior remodeling. A coincidence? There's no way to know for sure, of course. But I don't believe so. I was so busy I never met any of the neighbors to tell them what I was doing. I believe it was the energy of "fixing up" that was spreading from house to house. It all started with one person taking action and it caught on from there.

Our life goals are set in motion by the action of taking the first step, which initially starts as a mere thought. Once we focus on what we want, our unconscious mind creates the way for it to happen one action at a time, and one idea at a time. Ultimately, our dreams really can come true.

"Nothing happens until something moves."
Albert Einstein, Nobel Prize winner, physics

Why taking action is so important

Taking action is the most important aspect of creating the life you want. Anyone can have a dream, but without proper action a dream can end up becoming a source of regret. There are countless stories of people who came up with ideas for inventtions or books that were never patented or pursued. Later they discovered that someone else put a similar idea into production. One person misses out on contributing to the world and gaining financial independence for themselves and their families. The other person ends up becoming a millionaire and lives a completely different life, all because of one important difference. The person who has courage and takes action usually ends up succeeding.

After you read your Dream Cards, set an intention to take at least one action step every day toward your dream. Mornings are a great time to take a few seconds to write at least one action step that you intend to take that day. You can write it on a note card or a piece of paper. Keep your written action step with you or put it in a place where you will see it throughout the day. If you write more than one action step per day, make sure to accomplish at least one of the actions so you are always moving your plan forward. Setting a daily intention to take action works well even if you only actively pursue your dream five days a week and have weekends off.

"You snooze, you lose."
A popular 20th century phrase

Part Four
Creating more money in your life

Life costs money. Even if we wish it wasn't so, it's a reality we encounter every day. Having money is necessary to pursue our dreams as well as the basics of life like food and shelter. The creation of money is something you can achieve through your own efforts or with the help of others. Loans are often necessary to attend a college or a vocational school. Not everyone is fortunate enough to have a scholarship or someone paying for their education. School loans are "good" debt.

When you write about your financial future, write about how you will be earning and spending the money that will be coming in. It might feel lofty, phony, or delusional to you on some level; keep writing anyway. Remember the "how" part of Writing Your Future will evolve over time through research and by talking to others. First, your job is to solidify what you want to have happen.

In your mastermind group you could ask, "Who do you know who knows somebody who___." When you are given a name, a phone number, or an email address, be sure to take action. Be prepared with your specific questions or presentation when you make contact. People will appreciate that you are considerate.

> **"The mind is just another muscle."**
> Ted Turner, CNN founder and philanthropist

Eliminating fears and doubts around money

Our minds are so powerful they may create according to our thoughts, and by our spoken words and written words. By thinking about what you say before you say it, you will re-train your mind to think in a more positive way.

If you are continually fearful and worried about money, you may be creating more lack and scarcity. It's important not to focus or even to talk about not having enough or being in debt. Instead, write a plan for creating extra income and a plan for cutting back on spending. It's only a thought, and a thought can be changed. What do you want? What are you willing to give up in order to achieve what you want?

Some writing examples about money

I am spending my money wisely.
I only buy things I need.
I am careful and conscious of my spending.
I easily pay all my bills.
I always have enough money.
I am grateful for my job bonus or pay raise.
Extra money comes to me in unexpected ways.
I am a good steward of money.
I easily save money for my dreams.

Tip: Try using a blank check register and keeping a running total of what you're spending every month in different areas. This will help to keep you on target for your financial dreams.

Creating more wealth and eliminating debt

If creating debt is something you are struggling with, you could write something like this:

I only buy things I absolutely need.
I am always aware of my spending.
I am writing down all my expenditures.
I always have money to pay my bills on time.
I am on a cash only weekly allowance of____.
I easily stay within my expense budget of___.
I am so happy to be paying off_____ and _____.

Other money affirmations could be:

I save___ per week by bringing lunch from home.
I am so happy to be paying off my bill of_____.
I easily save_____ for my dream of___.
I am earning extra money by_____.
I am putting an extra_____ towards my mortgage every month.

Most of us get into debt one day at a time and that is exactly how we will eliminate it. A large part of spending has to do with awareness and setting limits on purchases. I have a friend who brings a calculator and only a certain amount of money to the grocery store each week. She ended up losing 20 pounds in three months as she eliminated the costly junk food she used to purchase.

Tip: Do NOT write "I'm getting out of debt by ______." Your mind imprints the word DEBT. Make sure all the words of your writing are positive
i.e.; "I easily pay off all my bills by the end of_____."

Beliefs about money

Money can really improve the lives of so many around the world, especially in Third World countries. Money can also greatly improve our own health and well-being. Much of what we believe about money gets ingrained in us from people we have spent time listening to and observing. Some common beliefs we may have heard about the rich are:

Rich people must be dishonest to earn so much.
Rich people don't give enough money to charity.
Rich people don't deserve that much money.
Rich people are selfish.
Rich people are greedy.

When you say these things about others, you are really saying it about yourself. That would translate to the idea that you don't deserve more money. There really is enough abundance for all of us. But first, you must believe it to be true.

Some people have created a life pattern of just barely getting by. This is called a "scarcity consciousness." By dwelling on thoughts of scarcity and not having enough, you only increase the odds that you will continue in the same pattern. Another common belief is that you have to work hard to make money. Though it is often true, there are many people who are well paid who do not work hard. However, if you believe that you must work hard, then you will unconsciously find ways to make it true for you.

Gratitude increases the speed of money into your life

Money has the power to change the world, and to change your world in particular. Notice how much easier it comes into your life and how much farther it goes when you are aware of your spending, earning, saving, and giving. Money has the power to help make your dreams, and the dreams of others come true.

Another great way to attract more money is to be grateful for the money you have earned or the money that has been given to you. Make a list of bonuses, gift money, or even money you found that has occurred in your life. There are millions of people every day who have money come to them easily. Intend to be one of them and you will increase the odds that it can happen for you as well.

You must believe in your heart and mind that you deserve happiness as well as financial prosperity. If you believe you need to be punished for every transgression you have committed, or if you believe you are unworthy, your unconscious mind will draw you to situations that can make you "right." By practicing new ways of thinking, eventually you will notice those doubting and unforgiving thoughts are just not coming to your mind as often, indeed, if at all.

> **"The more grateful you are, the more you will attract things to be grateful for."**
> Jack Canfield, author

Other Money affirmations

My income is always increasing.
Money comes to me from unexpected sources.
I deserve to have financial prosperity.
I happily share my financial abundance.
I am conscious of my spending and giving.
I am making good choices with money.

We can barter and trade services but it's a fact that life costs money. It's so easy to do, but complaining about gas, food, and housing prices will only deplete your life energy. Dwelling on things over which you have no control can leave you feeling drained. Consider putting your energy into writing a financial plan and Writing Your Future.

Start writing about how money could come into your life, but no pipe dreams. Yes, people can win the lottery, or have an inheritance, but for the most part, people earn their money. Don't be concerned if you don't have many details of the "how" figured out. As you get more involved in Writing Your Future the "how" will reveal itself day by day. Your unconscious mind will work behind the scenes to give you clues and steps on how to reach your goals. You must discover what you want before your mind can work on "how."

"My philosophy is that only you are responsible for your life, but doing the best at this moment puts you in the best place for the next moment."
Oprah Winfrey, philanthropist and television host

What will your dream cost?

Roughly how much will your "dream" cost? What will it cost you in time, energy, money, and sacrifice? What are you willing to give up in order to achieve your goal? Are you willing to give up watching television or being on the internet and then investing that time in your dream? Are you willing to get up early to work on your goal?

Write down some ideas for making more money that you can put towards your dream. You might need to talk to ten different banks or individuals before you get funding for your dream. You may have to seek loans from several groups of people. Don't give up. Ask for advice on how to improve your business plan and keep your vision in front of you at all times. Eventually, you will be likely to succeed.

Writing about your financial dreams

Start with a future date. Make it a realistic timeline. Don't put undue pressure on yourself. You would not want to give yourself six months to have a book published and a website up and running. Write ideas about how you might achieve your financial dreams. Allow time for the "seeds" you are planting to blossom. Remember, there's a growing season for everything.

"The three keys for success are being at the right place, knowing you are there, and taking action."
Ray Kroc, founder of McDonald's

From poverty to millionaire publisher: Marc Allen's story

Marc Allen is an author and the co-founder of the New World Library which publishes books by Deepak Chopra, Richard Carlson, Eckhart Tolle, Shakti Gawain and others. Here he tells his true life story.

The pivotal moment in my life was on my 30th birthday. For all of my adult life I lived on the brink of poverty in a ramshackle apartment just barely getting by. I knew things needed to change, but here's the catch. I did not want to have to work hard to achieve my dreams. I wanted to accomplish everything I set out to do in a relaxed and easy manner. I picked up a piece of paper and a pen and wrote the following list.

My ideal scene: In a relaxed and easy manner,

I own a publishing house.
I am a published author.
I don't work Mondays or mornings.
I work when I feel like it.
I work less than 40 hours a week.

At the time Marc Allen wrote his ideal scene he had no money, no family support, no real contacts, and no knowledge of publishing. Marc started a publishing company that year printing and selling small booklets. Later he expanded his business into publishing books.

Marc emphasizes that it wasn't easy for the first five years. His company endured a period of struggle which included the bankruptcy of the distributing company that was hired to deliver the books. He was not paid for thousands of books.

With a clear written vision in front of him, after the fifth year of business, the company was really starting to thrive. The fourth book that Marc published was called *Creative Visualization.* It went on to sell millions of copies. Marc is the author of *The Millionaire Course* and *Type Z: the Lazy Man's Guide to Success.* He credits writing his future to redirecting his life to a new and better direction. Marc Allen is now 60 years old and is living the life of his dreams.

"Imagination is the preview of life's coming attractions."
Albert Einstein, Nobel Prize winner, physics

You can still achieve many of your goals even if you don't earn more money

Sometimes our goals can still be achieved even if we don't end up making more money. No matter what your income level, there are always places to cut back on spending and then put the money you've saved towards your life dreams. You could also concentrate on those dreams that don't cost a lot of money. Losing weight is a goal that costs nothing when you use books and resources from the public library to assist you. Eating less will cost less, and walking is free.

The following are possible ways you can reduce spending: limit eating out in restaurants, get movies from the library instead of renting, reduce cable television channels, eliminate junk food, cigarettes or alcohol, buy food on sale or with coupons. You could also trade clothes with friends, buy clothes on sale or at a consignment shop. You could reduce the money spent on gas by carpooling, using public transportation or reducing driving time. Only you will know all the areas you can eliminate expenses.

If you are not in a position to change jobs or to add to your income, you can still achieve your dreams by cutting back on spending, or by putting on a yard sale and selling things on Ebay. Write down the amount of money you are intending to bring in. If you aren't comfortable writing down a specific number, write something like: *October is a huge money month for me.*

People who set a goal to get things for FREE

It is possible to obtain things at no cost, especially if you set an intention to do so. Why not dream big and be open to receiving a gift? Many people find great pleasure in helping someone else's dream come true. There are many groups on the internet that focus on recycling and helping people to give each other things for free such as www.freecycle.org.

A friend of mine wanted a new black leather couch. He cut out a picture from a furniture store flyer and put it on his Dream Board. He also taped a picture of a couch on a Dream Jar. Every week he deposited $20 in his jar in order to save for the couch. Two months later, he noticed his neighbor down the street had put a FREE sign on a black leather couch in good condition. Now he's using the money he saved for one of his other dreams.

Whether your goal is to be given something big or something small, it won't happen until you decide what you want to be given. Micah, a family friend, created a FREE wish list. He was involved with racing cars in Hawaii and decided he wanted to be given a race car for free. One year later, Micah was given a race car worth thousands of dollars in exchange for several hours of his time doing welding on the gate of the car owner's home.

"One man's junk is another's man treasure."
A 20th century expression

The drip system

In the funny movie, "What about Bob?" Richard Dreyfuss plays a psychiatrist who writes a book about taking "baby steps" to conquer fear and uses those principles to help his patient, Bill Murray. The movie chronicled a man's journey out of mental illness when he took just small steps to redirect his life.

The drip system is just like the "baby steps" program. Dripping involves taking a small action toward your dream. One idea in your life can start a chain reaction of movement with your dreams. If you drip on your life goals, you are nourishing your dreams. Eventually, the seeds you have sown can become a finished goal. But it all starts with the "dripping" process.

Reading your Dream Cards and looking at your Dream Board with a positive and expectant mind set can be the daily activity that helps you to "drip" on your goals. Every action you take, however small, will plant seeds toward your future dream fulfillment.

What dreams can you start dripping on today?

"You gain strength, courage, and confidence by every experience in which you really stop to look fear in the face. You are able to say to yourself. I have lived through this horror. "I can take the next thing that comes along. You must do the thing you think you cannot do."

Eleanor Roosevelt, Former First Lady

21 days to the fulfillment of your dreams

You must be willing to take steps, however small at first, to achieve your dreams. 21 days seems to be the magic number for creating a habit. This seems to be true whether we decide to start exercising everyday, reading an inspirational book, or creating whatever new habit we are planning to integrate into our lives on a daily basis. It starts with a commitment and then taking action to keep the promise.

In 21 days your life can be moving in a wonderful new direction. In 21 days you can be further along in a college class or vocational training. In 21 days you can be a step closer to saving money for your dream or exercising and losing weight. Every action you take each day toward your dream builds and builds until one day you have completion.

Set an intention to write your future, review your Dream Cards, or look through your Life Box just a few minutes a day for 21 days without a break. From then on try to work the program every day. The more consistent you are with "dripping" on your life goals, and checking off small steps, the sooner your dreams can become reality. Create a daily routine and then stick with it to maximize your success. Remember to take action steps towards your dream when you are at your best, rested and energetic.

"80% of success is just showing up."
Woody Allen, director, writer, actor

The importance of keeping agreements

If 80% of success is showing up, the other 20% of success could be in keeping one's agreements. In today's society, there are many people who do not keep their word. This may explain why lawsuits are so common. People make agreements and then decide it's too hard to do what they say they will do. By keeping your agreements, you will stand out in the crowd.

How many times has someone said, "I'll call you or do______" and they didn't? It happens every day, even in business circles where one would think keeping a promise would be more likely. By doing what you say you will do, you will find that your confidence in yourself will grow. You will feel proud of yourself for keeping your word. When you keep your agreements with others, you will find it easier to keep your agreements with yourself to work on accomplishing your dreams.

You will discover that as you work hard to always do what you say you will do, others will be likely to think of you in a positive way. Keeping agreements builds trust and people will know they can count on you. This is especially important today as people want to know you will perform as agreed. By keeping promises, your reputation will very likely be a positive one.

"The nearest way to glory is to strive to be what you wish to be thought to be."
Socrates, Greek philosopher

The importance of discipline

Discipline has become an unpleasant word for many of us. Our inner child screams, "You can't tell me what to do!" or "You can't make me!" Webster's dictionary defines discipline as: "Training that adjusts self-control, efficiency." A large part of discipline is directly tied into habit and routine.

Creating a routine for doing anything requires discipline. You can take action, no matter how small, to bring yourself closer to your goals. The important part of the Writing Your Future method is to read your Dream Cards every day and to take even small steps towards their attainment. It could be something as simple as making a phone call, doing some research for a few minutes on the internet, ordering a book, going to the library and so on. Action is always essential for the attainment of your life wishes.

Many of the "baby steps" to your dream truly do not take up large amounts of time. It is discipline and habit that create the space for you to do what you need to do to bring our dreams to fruition. Be open for the "how" of your dreams to unfold one thought or day at a time. It may take months or years for your dream to come together. By keeping your vision in your mind and with the development of a plan, you will likely succeed.

"Discipline yourself today,
so tomorrow you can have it all."
Brian Buffini, real estate coach

Part Five
Giving back to Maximize your Success

There was a wonderful movie called "Pay it Forward" with Kevin Spacey, Helen Hunt and Haley Joel Osment. It showed how one person's giving can create a domino effect of other people doing good deeds. The concept of tithing works like that. There is a beautiful energy that comes from giving, but we have to do it, to feel it.

Money has the power to change lives

Money equals freedom to many people. But if you don't feel comfortable having more money, find a cause that interests you and donate to them. With the internet, it's very easy to research different reputable charities. The Nobel Peace Prize winner of 2006 was Prof. Muhammad Yunus who started Grameen Bank. They give loans of $50-200 so people can break out of poverty and start their own bus-nesses. Amazingly, the payback rate has been close to one hundred percent. When you give to someone, consider whether you are giving them a hand out or a hand up.

Giving away time and money can actually bring more money into your life

The best way to ensure an ongoing flow of abundance into your life is to share with others part of what you receive. Perhaps you might consider giving to an organization that has inspired or helped you in the past.

Some people commit to tithing, which is giving 10% of your gross or net income to a worthy cause. Multi-millionaire writers Mark Victor Hansen, Robert Allen, Jack Canfield, and others credit their mega wealth to tithing first, and then reaping the rewards of giving later. They are committed to giving from the abundance that comes in. The key is giving without resentment or expectation. You will eventually receive, but often it is weeks or months later and usually from someone different than those to whom you gave.

It may feel overwhelming to give away that much money as most of us were not raised with the 10% tithing concept. Consider donating 1% of your income to a cause that interests you. As you see the results in your own life, increase your giving from there. Time tithing can be another generous form of giving. Consider giving even an hour or two a week volunteering at a shelter, food bank, or any other charitable organization. Helping out a friend or family member is another way to serve. Stick with it for three months. I promise you will reap the rewards of giving.

Mark Hansen, co-author of the *Chicken Soup for the Soul* series, teaches a great concept about money. He encourages people to save 10%, to give 10% and invest 10% from every paycheck. *The Miracle of Tithing*, also by Mark Hansen, has stories of people who were in serious debt and how their lives drastically improved once they committed to tithing in spite of their debt. This very short book will change your thinking about giving. It can be purchased at:

www.markvictorhansen.com

Remember that every dollar makes a difference to someone in the world who is going without food, running water, clothes or necessary healthcare. There are many stories about how the act of giving brought the giver even more money than they donated.

> **"Tithing always pays the best dividends."**
> John Templeton Marks, philanthropist

One man's story of giving and receiving

Steven Zale is an award winning jewelry designer who is involved with Operation Smile children's charity. Many people wear his jewelry like model Rachel Hunter and other celebrities. He and a business partner agreed to split the $150,000 cost of an Operation Smile surgical mission. At the last minute his business partner backed out. As a new manufacturer, Steven's funds were limited and the $75,000 he had committed was a big stretch.

Steven Zale experienced firsthand the life changing procedures at a surgical mission in Fortaleza, Brazil. He was so moved by his interaction with the children that he was more determined than ever to fund an entire mission. Steven had no idea where the money was going to come from, but he made an agreement anyway to give Operation Smile the entire $150,000.

Steven Zale said, "After I signed papers with Operation Smile, it was like an invisible force entered my business. Huge business opportunities came my way. Within a few months of my agreement with Operation Smile, I was awarded a multi-million dollar contract to manufacture the jewelry line of a Fortune 500 company. All I can say is when you give, it comes back to you, sometimes far beyond anything you could ever imagine."

Steven Zale's website is www.zalemark.com

In my own life, I volunteered as a music therapist for the elderly aunt and uncle of a girlfriend. At one time, her aunt had been a concert pianist but after having a stroke she was no longer able to play. I drove 1.5 hours roundtrip to play the piano many times for them at no charge. Even though I did feel a bit guilty for taking time away from my real estate career, I just trusted and believed that it would come back to me eventually in some form.

Did it ever come back! After my two new friends passed away, their family listed for sale three of their homes with me. One family member even gave me a generous bonus separate from the real estate commission. I shared my musical abilities not because I could get something, but because I knew I could enrich the lives of two people who were lonely and homebound.

Trust that when you give you will eventually receive, and you will. It's important not to have expectations of things coming to you immediately after a donation of time, money, or goodwill. You've planted seeds in the circle of life and you must give them time to grow.

John Crean credits being "a giver" as his key to his life's success. Shortly after he donated one million dollars to help build a large church, the stock in his company increased in value over twenty percent.

"The more you give, the more you get back."
John Crean, philanthropist, manufacturer

A man who left Microsoft to change the world

John Wood was a high level executive at Microsoft when he went on a hiking expedition in Nepal that forever changed his life. He came across make-shift schools in small villages that had only a handful of tattered books that were kept locked up. This experience had a profound effect on John. He told one of the teachers in the village that he would be back next year with a supply of books for the children.

Through research, John discovered that there were 800 million people who were illiterate in the world. With the help of his parents, John started a book drive and was able to deliver three thousand books the following year. The teacher told John Wood that many people came to his village in Nepal and promised to come back or to send help, but no one ever did.

John made the decision to leave Microsoft in 1999 to work full-time in bringing books to Third World Countries by starting a non-profit foundation called Room to Read. With the help of many generous benefactors, he has raised funds to build 3600 libraries and donated 2.8 million books to children around the world. John Wood exemplifies how a caring heart, focus, and action can make a difference in the world.

www.roomtoread.org

"Be the change you want to see in the world."
Mahatma Gandhi, peace activist

One teenager's dream to end slavery

Most people think the average teenager isn't capable of much beyond hanging with their friends and wasting time. But 15 year old Zach Hunter isn't your average teenager.

Since the age of 12, he has been busy trying to end slavery around the globe. Most people think that slavery has been over for a long time, but there are more people bound in slavery now than at any of the times we read about in our history books. Zach is working to end slavery and free the men, women, and children who are being held against their will.

He discovered that there are 27 million people living in indentured servitude, half of them are children who had been sold into slavery by their parents to pay off debts. In addition, nearly 17,500 people are trafficked across international borders each year for the purpose of being slaves.

Zach Hunter wants teens and twenty-somethings to know that even though they are young, they can still make a difference in the world. He created a way for all of us to abolish slavery by asking people to give their loose change, quarters, dimes, nickels, pennies to loosen the chains of bondage for millions of people.

www.theamazingchange.com

"We're too young to know that some things are impossible, so we will do them anyway."
William Pitt, author

Part Six
Summary of how to write your future

I used to know a directionless man whom I had met in a part time restaurant job. His name was Peter. His favorite saying in life was, "You never know where you are going until you get there." He was right. He never knew where he was going. He had no oar in the water, no compass, no direction. Peter just wandered from job to job never thinking about anything beyond the next payday.

Many of us are like that at some point in our lives. Some of us are lucky enough to meet someone who influences us. Some just find that they are good at something like sales or a creative pursuit. But for the rest of us there needs to be a beginning from the inside. We need a spark which will ignite a path to happiness and a life full of returns. The spark has to be held on to and it needs to be adhered to. It needs above all else to be reduced to writing so that we can enlarge it to a dream. We all are capable of pursuing a dream, but first, let's write it down. With the help of our imagination and belief in ourselves, we can create our future one thought, one word, and one action at a time.

> **"If you don't know where you're going, you'll wind up someplace else."**
> Yogi Berra, former Yankees baseball coach

It's been said that the pursuit of pleasure and the avoidance of pain are primary motivators of human behavior. Procrastination is a form of pain avoidance and can be brought on by fear or a perfectionist attitude. Some people may not take action unless they can do something really well or they don't want to do it at all. Writing Your Future works best when you take action steps, no matter how small or how imperfect, as soon as you write and set your goals.

Other people have difficulty with the goal writing process because they believe they can't do something and they give up before trying. Henry Ford said, "If you believe you can, you can. If you believe you can't, you can't." If you proclaim your limitations and obstacles for your life, they can become true for you by becoming a self-fulfilled prophecy.

If your predominant thoughts about your future are those of doubt and fear, you must take action to quiet those negative thoughts in your mind. The local libraries have self-help books and tapes that can assist you in eliminating negative self talk. Having a positive vision for your life goals, uninterrupted as much as possible by doubting thoughts, is essential for having your dreams come to fruition.

"The difference between what we do, and what we are capable of doing, would suffice to solve most of the world's problems."
Mahatma Gandhi, peace activist

The five important steps to attaining your goal

1. Know what you want.
2. See and feel yourself doing it.
3. Write Dream Cards and journal about it.
4. Believe you deserve it.
5. Take action steps to achieve your goal.

Be specific about what you want

First, you have to decide what you want. As you begin taking action steps, however small, you are in the process of completing your dream. It's good to put an end date to your goal even if it's five or ten years in the future. Many of our goals will take years to accomplish. Allowing adequate time to achieve your life wish is essential, otherwise you can become stressed and frustrated.

Once you decide what you want to achieve, your unconscious mind will work behind the scenes to help you. In January 2000, I decided I wanted to be a writer. At that time, my writing skills were limited and I had never written anything for any type of publication. However, I believed that with education and practice, I could learn to be a writer. As I took writing classes and practiced writing, I was in the process of becoming a writer. Six years later I became a published writer just as I set out to be.

"When one of your dreams come true, you begin to look at the others more carefully."
Anonymous

Additional resources to help you

* *Hire a life coach or a mentor.*
* *Join or start a mastermind group.*
* *Do research at the library or on the internet.*
* *Ask people if they know anyone who knows about whatever you are trying to do.*
* *Attend a class, seminar or convention.*

Make your statements short and add a descriptive word like easily, happily, enjoying, liking, loving.

I am easily learning Spanish.
I am enjoying my new job.
I am happily driving a ____.

The three step process of any goal

I want to____.
I am in the process of becoming/doing/having____.
I am ____.

First you have to know what you want to achieve. You have to first picture your dream in your mind before it can become reality. The second step begins as you are writing down ways to obtain your goal and visualizing yourself doing whatever it is you want to do. At this point, you are in the process of working on your goal even though you may not actually be achieving it yet. The second step is the longest part of the process so be patient. The third step is the actual attainment of your goal.

Some of what you are writing may feel like a lie. For example, if you have written a Dream Card that says: *I am healthy and at a perfect weight of____.* But in reality you are fifty pounds away from your goal.

You could be having thoughts like *"that's a lie, you're really_____."*

If it seems like too much of an untruth and you are not comfortable with an "I am" statement,
I recommend you adjust your wording to something like this:

I am now in the process of becoming _____weight.

It is not a lie to say that you are in the process of becoming or doing something. In reality, until your goal is actually completed, you truly are in the process of doing anything.

If losing weight is your goal, you may consider cutting a picture out of a magazine of a smaller person and superimpose a headshot of yourself over the body. You could also put a real photo of yourself at a lower weight on the board. With a plan, action, and the passage of time, you will eventually be similar to the picture.

I want to be healthy and energetic at _____weight.
I am in the process of being ____weight.
I am healthy and energetic at _____weight.

I want to be the top salesperson this month.
I am in the process of becoming the top salesperson this month.
I am the top salesperson this month.

Tip: If you want to lose weight, check out this website.
www.toxinrelease.isagenix.com
There are many people who lost 50-100 lbs on this medical doctor endorsed program.

Five minute daily routine for Writing Your Future

1. Start and end your day by reading your Dream Cards with your written goals. Your unconscious mind is most accessible at these times.

2. Look at your Dream Board or Dream Book at least one minute a day while imagining what it will feel like to have achieved your dreams.

3. Monitor your thoughts. Believe you deserve what you are writing about. See yourself doing whatever it is you want to do. Feel what it would be like if you have achieved your goal.

4. Every morning write down on a piece of paper or a note card at least one action you will take by the end of the day to move your dream forward. Carry it with you or place it in a place where you can see it throughout the day.

5. Reflect on the day, recalling things to be grateful for. Write down one positive thing that happened on the Gratitude Log. Forgive yourself and others for things that didn't go the way you intended.

Tip: Say to yourself often: "I believe all the information on how to achieve my dream is coming to me one thought at a time."

Focus on three goals for each life category

Money and possessions
1. ______________________________
2. ______________________________
3. ______________________________

Career, Education, Job
1. ______________________________
2. ______________________________
3. ______________________________

Love, Friends, Family
1. ______________________________
2. ______________________________
3. ______________________________

Health, Fitness, Appearance
1. ______________________________
2. ______________________________
3. ______________________________

Dreams and Aspirations
1. ______________________________
2. ______________________________
3. ______________________________

Fun and Vacations
1. ______________________________
2. ______________________________
3. ______________________________

Spiritual and Contribution
1. ______________________________
2. ______________________________
3. ______________________________

Things you can do weekly or monthly to help you reach your goal.

1. On your 101 things you want to do in your lifetime list, from time to time, write down new things you want to do. Let your mind consider all the different times of your life the 20's, 30's, 40's, and beyond.

2. Review your 101 things I'm grateful for in my life list. Remember to include specific events and lucky occurrences. When you feel discouraged, refer back to this list to remind yourself of the good that has happened in the past. Wonderful events happened before and they can happen again.

3. In your Writing Your Future Journal write about your life as if it is already happening. Write in the present tense with a future date. It could be one month, one year, three years, five, ten, or even twenty years out.

4. Open up your Life Box and read through your Victory Cards, personal emails and cards with a positive message and other uplifting contents. Feel how appreciated and loved you are as evidenced by thank you notes, emails, and other memorabilia in your Life Box.

Tip: Designate a time weekly or monthly to review any of those lists such as the first Sunday morning of every month, every Friday night or whatever day that works best for you.

Taking yourself from a possibility to a defined goal

Write your goal in one sentence as if it is currently happening. Use an adjective like happily, easily etc. Remember, feelings are the reason we do anything.

3 Important steps to working with Dream Cards

* Repeat the words of your Dream Card in your mind or say them out loud.

* See yourself doing or having your dream.

* Feel the feelings you would feel if your dream came true.

Did you know that an airliner flying from Los Angeles to New York is off course at different times throughout the flight? The pilot makes adjustments that eventually get the plane to the final destination. As you are in the process of making your life wish come true, you too will be making adjustments along the way. You may decide to change or eliminate a particular goal after getting more information, or you might extend the end date. By refocusing and getting more information and the necessary tools to complete your goal, you will ultimate reach your destination just like the plane.

"Never Give up, NEVER give up."
Winston Churchill, British Prime Minister

Taking action on the incomplete areas in your life

Make a list of the things around your home, yard, or workplace that you want or need to do. Perhaps there are closets and shelves that need to be organized and deep down it drains your energy when you think about it. Maybe there are thank you notes or calls, apologies, monies you owe, or are owed you that need to be addressed. Perhaps you might have to break a promise or renegotiate one. Let the other person know you can't keep a commitment as soon as you are aware of it. Being a person of integrity will help you maintain your life energy for your goals.

You could take action on your list of incompletes by starting with the items that only take a few minutes. Maybe you can address and stamp an envelope of the Thank You note you want to send out, or draft and save an email. Most incomplete tasks take very little time but give back so much in terms of energy, peace of mind, and a sense of accomplishment. You will be amazed at how much better you feel when you tackle, one by one, the incomplete issues in your life. You may find that you regain energy and focus that will open up the space for new and exciting things to come into your life.

"Thank you" are the two most important words of any language."
Daniel Peralta, teacher

One page summary of how to Write your Future
Beginning the day

1. Lay in bed for a few minutes and look at your Dream Board on the wall and feel what it would feel like to have accomplished all you have on your board.

2. Keep your Dream Cards next to your bed for easy access. Repeat slowly, the words of each Dream Card in your mind. Pause for 3-10 seconds between cards and feel the feelings you would feel if you achieved your dream.

3. On a piece of paper or a note card write 1-3 things you are going to do today to research or "drip" on your dream. Carry the paper with you or put it in a place where you will see it.

Ending the day

1. Write something you are grateful for, or something positive that happened today on your Gratitude Log.

2. Read your Dream Cards again, pausing for 3-10 seconds between cards.

3. Ask your unconscious mind to reveal the next step to take to make your dream come to fruition.

The items listed here will take only a few minutes a day. From the tools detailed in this book, create the Writing Your Future plan that works best for you.

The importance of persistence and hard work

Be open to all of life's possibilities for easy opportunities. However, statistics show that many people do have to work hard to achieve job advancement, education, or whatever their life wishes are. Don't be afraid of hard work. If your dreams are important to you, you will do what is necessary to take action on your life goals.

Writer, actor, director Sylvester Stallone wrote the screenplay for the film "Rocky." His dream was to have the lead role in the movie. Initially the screenplay was turned down by over one hundred production companies before someone agreed to buy it as long as Sylvester wasn't in it. This did not match the vision he had for himself. He continued speaking to other film makers. A production company finally agreed to buy the screenplay for very little money when Sylvester insisted he star in the film. In 1976 "Rocky" won the Academy Award for best Picture. Sylvester Stallone was nominated for Academy Awards for best original screenplay and best actor.

Imagine if Stallone had given up after the first few rejections or even after the fiftieth? Sylvester Stallone exemplifies the importance of hard work, persistence, and belief in one's self.

"You can't hire someone else to do your pushups for you."
Jim Rohn, motivational speaker

The importance of self-encouragement

On life's journey, each of us makes mistakes and we sometimes say or do the wrong things. It's not always easy, but the key is to remember to learn the lesson and to forgive yourself and others. It's important to avoid dwelling on past mistakes. There is nothing you can do now to change what happened, so for your own peace of mind, you must let it go. Once optimism and creative problem solving become part of your daily life, you will realize how much more energy you have living in the present and planning your future. Whatever part of the Writing Your Future method you choose as your favorite tool, you will very likely have success with your goals if you stick with it every day.

It's a great practice at the end of the day to recall all the things you are grateful for in your life, or in the day. Remember to compliment yourself for the things you said or did right. If things did not go the way you wanted them to, remember, tomorrow is another day. It is belief, a plan, and most importantly action and persistence that work together to bring your life wish to the next level. Take even one small step towards the attainment of your life goals every day, and eventually you will discover that your dreams really can come true.

"If we did all that we are capable of doing, we would literally astound ourselves."
Albert Einstein

Afterword from the author

Take time for yourself each day to dream and think about how you want your life to be. By believing anything is truly possible and by taking small action steps toward your dreams, they will very likely come to pass. Your goal may take longer than your initial set date. If you are continually getting closer to your dream, you are on the right track. Give yourself permission to extend your dates as needed as you come across new information on how to achieve your goals. Remember, you will have the best chance for achieving your dreams if you are a person of integrity, compassion, commitment, and persistence.

I want everyone to have the tools to create the life of their dreams. I thank you in advance for telling others about his book and website. I give substantial discounts on large quantity purchases of the book and workbook. I am also available to speak to your group or organization.

I want to include your success story in my next book called *Coming True*. Please write me and tell me how these techniques worked for you. I look forward to hearing your stories!

colleen@writingyourfuture.com

"The journey of 1,000 miles starts with a single step."
Chinese proverb

What is Operation Smile?

Operation Smile was founded in 1982 by Dr. Bill Magee, a craniofacial surgeon, and his wife Kathy. They gathered a group of their friends and traveled to the Philippines to perform surgeries on children with facial deformities.

Dr. Magee and his wife were astounded by what they saw. People walked hundreds of miles to come to the Operation Smile hospital site. Three hundred children arrived, but Dr. Magee and his staff could only help forty children. They knew they would have to come back the following year. As word spread about the surgeries, more children came the following year and Operation Smile was born.

Like the saying, "Give a man a fish and you feed him for a day, teach him to fish and you feed him for a lifetime." Operation Smile's mission is to train surgeons in each of the countries they visit, so those surgeons can perform the surgeries themselves.

Since 1982, Operation Smile and their volunteer doctors and nurses have corrected thousands of children's faces in twenty five countries. Lack of funds prevents Operation Smile from going to more countries and helping more children. There are thousands of children waiting for facial surgery worldwide.

www.operationsmile.org

101 Things I would like to do in my lifetime

Many people take months or years to write 101 possibilities. Take your time and dream big!

1. ______________________________
2. ______________________________
3. ______________________________
4. ______________________________
5. ______________________________
6. ______________________________
7. ______________________________
8. ______________________________
9. ______________________________
10. ______________________________
11. ______________________________
12. ______________________________
13. ______________________________
14. ______________________________
15. ______________________________
16. ______________________________
17. ______________________________
18. ______________________________
19. ______________________________
20. ______________________________
21. ______________________________
22. ______________________________
23. ______________________________
24. ______________________________
25. ______________________________
26. ______________________________
27. ______________________________
28. ______________________________
29. ______________________________
30. ______________________________
31. ______________________________

32. ______________________________
33. ______________________________
34. ______________________________
35. ______________________________
36. ______________________________
37. ______________________________
38. ______________________________
39. ______________________________
40. ______________________________
41. ______________________________
42. ______________________________
43. ______________________________
44. ______________________________
45. ______________________________
46. ______________________________
47. ______________________________
48. ______________________________
49. ______________________________
50. ______________________________
51. ______________________________
52. ______________________________
53. ______________________________
54. ______________________________
55. ______________________________
56. ______________________________
57. ______________________________
58. ______________________________
59. ______________________________
60. ______________________________
61. ______________________________
62. ______________________________
63. ______________________________
64. ______________________________
65. ______________________________
66. ______________________________
67. ______________________________
68. ______________________________

69. ____________________
70. ____________________
71. ____________________
72. ____________________
73. ____________________
74. ____________________
75. ____________________
76. ____________________
77. ____________________
78. ____________________
79. ____________________
80. ____________________
81. ____________________
82. ____________________
83. ____________________
84. ____________________
85. ____________________
86. ____________________
87. ____________________
88. ____________________
89. ____________________
90. ____________________
91. ____________________
92. ____________________
93. ____________________
94. ____________________
95. ____________________
96. ____________________
97. ____________________
98. ____________________
99. ____________________
100. ____________________
101. ____________________

101 Things I am grateful for in my life

Reflect back on your life and consider all the events and positive occurrences that have transpired. Add to this list as you think of the people, things, and events you appreciate.

1.____
2.____
3.____
4.____
5.____
6.____
7.____
8.____
9.____
10. ____
11. ____
12. ____
13. ____
14. ____
15. ____
16. ____
17. ____
18. ____
19. ____
20. ____
21. ____
22. ____
23. ____
24. ____
25. ____
26. ____
27. ____
28. ____
29. ____
30. ____

31. ______
32. ______
33. ______
34. ______
35. ______
36. ______
37. ______
38. ______
39. ______
40. ______
41. ______
42. ______
43. ______
44. ______
45. ______
46. ______
47. ______
48. ______
49. ______
50. ______
51. ______
52. ______
53. ______
54. ______
55. ______
56. ______
57. ______
58. ______
59. ______
60. ______
61. ______
62. ______
63. ______
64. ______
65. ______
66. ______
67. ______

68. ______________________________
69. ______________________________
70. ______________________________
71. ______________________________
72. ______________________________
73. ______________________________
74. ______________________________
75. ______________________________
76. ______________________________
77. ______________________________
78. ______________________________
79. ______________________________
80. ______________________________
81. ______________________________
82. ______________________________
83. ______________________________
84. ______________________________
85. ______________________________
86. ______________________________
87. ______________________________
88. ______________________________
89. ______________________________
90. ______________________________
91. ______________________________
92. ______________________________
93. ______________________________
94. ______________________________
95. ______________________________
96. ______________________________
97. ______________________________
98. ______________________________
99. ______________________________
100. ______________________________
101. ______________________________

Sample Daily Gratitude Log

It only takes a few seconds to write down one positive thing that happened each day. You can photocopy this page or create your own.

Monday ____________________________________

Tuesday ____________________________________

Wednesday ____________________________________

Thursday ____________________________________

Friday ____________________________________

Saturday ____________________________________

Sunday ____________________________________

Monday ____________________________________

Tuesday ____________________________________

Wednesday ____________________________________

Thursday ____________________________________

Friday ____________________________________

Saturday ____________________________________

Sunday ____________________________________

Recommended Reading

The magic of believing	Claude Bristol
As a man thinketh	James Allen
Gratitude: A Way of Life	Louise Hay
Chicken Soup for the Soul	Mark Hansen
(Living your dreams)	Jack Canfield
Success Principles	Jack Canfield
The Miracle of Tithing	Mark Hansen
The Power of Focus	Hewitt-Hansen-Canfield
The Millionaire Mind	Harv Eker
Think and Grow Rich	Napoleon Hill
Feel the Fear and do it anyway	Susan Jeffers
You'll see it when you believe it	Dr. Wayne Dyer
The Power of Intention	Dr. Wayne Dyer
Omega 3 Connection	Dr. Andrew Stoll
The Zone Diet	Dr. Barry Spears
Creative Visualization	Shakti Gawain
Write it Down, Make it Happen	Henriette Klauser
The Magic of thinking Big	David Schwartz
The Science of Getting Rich	Wallace Waddles
The Greatest Secret in the World	Og Mandino
There are no Limits	Danny Cox
The on-Purpose Person	Kevin McCarthy
What to say when you talk to yourself	Shad Helmstetter

Give the book Writing Your Future to people you know who want to have the life of their dreams. It's the perfect graduation or New Year's gift.

Yes, I want___copies of Writing your Future Books, plus $5 shipping for up to two books.

Washington State Residents:
Please add 8.9% sales tax to your order.

Book	$15.00	CD AudioBook	$10.00
Ebook	$10.00	Colored Dream Cards	$ 5.00

Please charge my VISA, Mastercard, American Express, Discover

Name ____

Organization ___________________________________

Address_______________________________________

City/State/Zip _________________________________

Phone ____

Card#_____________________________Exp Date _____

Security code (3 or 4 digits on the back of credit card) _______

Signature______________________________________

Please make your check or Money Order payable and mail the order form to:

Heart World Books
13016 2nd Ave SW
Burien, WA 98146

Call in your order to 206 250 3327
You can also order on our secure website
www.writingyourfuture.com
Fax your order to 1 800 695 8395

Here I am writing about my future

Here I am writing about my future

Here I am writing about my future

Here I am writing about my future

Here I am writing about my future

Here I am writing about my future

Here I am writing about my future

Here I am writing about my future

Here I am writing about my future

Here I am writing about my future

Here I am writing about my future

Here I am writing about my future

Printed in the United States
80075LV00002B/1-195

9 780979 525209